# Journey to the Promised Land

Omesha G.

Copyright © 2024 Omesha G.



ISBN: 9798869260000

Interior Design: Arilia Winn

# DEDICATION

This book is dedicated to anyone that feels as though their disobedience has disqualified them from the promise. God is patiently waiting to guide you back on track. Keep going, your promise awaits you.

# CONTENTS

# ACKNOWLEDGMENTS

Thank you to my grandparents. They supported me and wanted what was best for me during this transition and on this Journey.I wouldn't be who I am or where I am without them.

To my bestie, Takejah, and my Sister- Friends Bri, Teray and Azari. Thank you. Your prayers, support and love has held me up during the best of times and the worst of times. From weddings, to miscarriages to funerals and everything in-between you have been there. Because of you and God of course, I did not break.

To my Sisthers that became my sisters, thank you. I met you in the middle of transition but you all have shown nothing but love and support since day 1. Your sisterhood has helped me on this Journey.

To the head Sisther in charge, Kierra Sheard- Kelly. Your song "It Keeps Happening for me", was the catalyst for this book to be honest. Your song inspired the painting I did for you that I named "The Promised Land." which caused me to think about my own Promised Land. Your own Journey to Wifehood and Motherhood has shown me that it is possible and reminds me that God keeps his promises.

Last but not least, to my Pastor, Bill Russell Jr., and my Harvest City church family. Thank you. Being a Partner of this great church and a part of such a loving community of believers has been such a breath of fresh air on this Journey. It has made some of the darkest days a little brighter. Because of you I know that God is mindful of me.

# CHAPTER ONE

I was raised by my paternal grandparents. They took on the responsibility of caring for me from the time I was six months old. My mother and father were young when they conceived me. My father was 18 and my mother was 19 years old when I came into the world. I was my mother's 2nd child. I have an older sister that I would not meet until I was around 4 or 5 years old. I remember when my mom told me I had an older sister. I was ecstatic. She is five years older than me and didn't live too far from me. My grandparents planned to surprise me with a visit to meet her. Growing up, my favorite restaurant was Golden Corral, so they told me that's where we were going. But to my surprise we didn't pull up at Golden Corral, we pulled up in an unfamiliar place. It was someone's house, but who's?

Although the place was unfamiliar I wasn't afraid or nervous because I was with my grandparents. I always felt safe with them. When I was with them I felt like nothing bad could happen to me. We got out of the car and knocked on the door when a face I didn't recognize came to answer the door. We were at my sister's house, and I was there to meet her for the first time. I was raised as an only child, so I was so happy to have a big sister and to finally meet and get to know her. I remember hearing the people that were there talk and thinking they had a funny accent. My sister was raised in a place called Manteo that has very thick southern accents and they speak a little faster than what I was used to. My sister and I got along well so my grandparents and I stayed there for a few hours while I played and then it was time to leave. I wasn't sad to leave because I knew what was next, so I thought. I was having fun playing with my sister but, food over everything. I hadn't forgotten that they told me that we were going to Golden Corral, not realizing that it was just a decoy for the surprise. Although I was happy to have met my sister I was not happy about not going to my favorite restaurant. My joy quickly faded into disappointment as we drove past the city that held my favorite restaurant to our home way down in the country in a small town by the name of Pantego, North Carolina.

During the short time that I lived with my mom, my grandparents would allow my mom to stay over at their house with me. They would buy anything that my mom needed for me such as milk and diapers. I was their first grandchild. I'd like to think I was their pride and joy. My mom and I lived with my maternal grandmother across the bridge in a slightly bigger town called Belhaven. My father, who never felt quite comfortable with my mother's living arrangements, would frequently bring me home to his parents' house. The house that my mom lived in was very popular. It's where many people came to play cards and hang out, both men and women. As a first time dad, it made him a little uncomfortable to have his baby in that type of environment. Not necessarily unsafe, but not the ideal environment for a baby. My grandparents would get me for the weekend and take me back home to my mom and she'd say "sure is a lot of people in here." My grandmother would often wake up in the middle of the night and I would be right back in bed beside her leaving her confused because she knew she'd already taken me home. Not yet able to upend her life for a better environment, my mother asked my grandparents if they would keep me full time. With some initial hesitation, as they had one adult son and their youngest son about 5 years away from turning 18, my grandparents agreed to take me in. But not without making her promise not to later change her mind.

She kept her promise. I always knew my mother and never had any confusion as to who my parents were.

My mother was never too far away, but she knew my grandparents would do a better job at rearing me. When I was a little girl my grandmother would thank the Lord for giving me to her and I would say, "The Lord didn't give me to you, my mommy did." There were some weekends I would go stay with my mother. I liked to stay with her on occasion but there were times that I would quickly want to go home, sometimes even making up excuses such as "I have to do my homework" although I wasn't in school yet. My paternal grandaddy didn't, and still doesn't play about me. One weekend I went to stay with my mom, and I called my grandparents in the middle of the night wanting to go home. My grandma suggested they wait until the next morning to come and get me but my grandaddy wasn't having it. He said "she could be hungry or anything" so they came that night. There was nothing wrong, I just simply wanted to go home.

My maternal grandmother passed away when I was about 3 years old. After that my mom lived mostly with different relatives. When I was with my mom I didn't feel unsafe but my home with my grandparents was my safe place. It's where I felt most comfortable.

Though I loved being raised by my grandparents, there was a point that I noticed I was different. I was aware of the fact that I was one of the very few of my peers that didn't live with their parents. At one point it made me sad, and I briefly wanted to live with my mom. I wanted to know what it was like to live with your mom as I had never had that experience. I would go down the list of my peers trying to think of who lived with someone other than their mom too so that I didn't feel like such an odd ball. I would tell people that I was going to go live with my mom and my grandmother would quickly tell them "No she isn't." It wasn't in a rude way at all, but she knew that what I was going through was just a phase. My grandmother wasn't super strict, but I had a little more freedom with my mom. There was a little more to do while I was with her such as walking down the street with my cousins and peers or listening to more secular music. I was around a lot more kids my age as there weren't many kids where I lived and the ones that were there were mainly my boy cousins. All of that was fun but, just like my grandmother knew, the desire to live with my mom was short-lived. It was simply a phase.

I can't say that I've never felt any resentment towards my mom, because I have. In the way that I communicate best, through writing, I have written to her expressing how I felt about everything because at times it felt that she did more for others than she did for me. It sometimes felt that she never kept her word when it came to things she said she would do. But I have forgiven her. I can say that now, I hold no resentment towards her because she did the best she could with what she had. She later lived with her mom, but her grandmother raised her too. She often thanks me for never disrespecting her and I know she is grateful to my grandparents for taking me in. Though I'm sure that my mother has some regrets, I am confident that she made the right choice. She and my dad were the vehicles God used to birth me and for that I am grateful. I also know that I wouldn't be who I am today without the rearing of my grandparents.

God is strategic.

Even in things we may not understand, He works it for our good.

My dad and I grew up as what felt like siblings. When he moved out, I stayed. After he moved out he was still around. I would go spend weekends with him. I remember taking a road trip to New York with him. Growing up, I would go visit family in Maryland during the summer and he would drive me. When he lived closer or would come to visit he would take me to my little league practices. He'd take me shopping or give me money. Sometimes as a kid he would randomly give me $20.00, and I just knew I was ballin! So, although we didn't live under the same roof he was present, attending every big moment in my life. But while we lived under the same roof, what Ella, my grandmother, said held more power than anyone else's, even daddy's.

There was no place like my grandparent's house. Being raised by my grandparents came with stability. I lived in the same house from six months until I went off to college. It's still the place that I call home. The place that wraps me like a warm hug when life is getting the best of me. When I had my first miscarriage I knew that once I got "home" everything would be okay. Even if only for a few days. I had all the things I needed and even things that I wanted. Some would even say I'm spoiled but I say I'm blessed. Being raised by my grandparents gave me a close family. Family that has been there for the many stages of my life. They were there for sports events, various graduations from kindergarten to college, weddings and even funerals. It also meant being raised next door to my cousin who is also my best friend. My best friend was being raised by her grandmother, my grandmother's sister while her mom finished college. We grew up together. Our grandparents went everywhere together, and they usually bought us the same toys for birthdays and holidays. Being that my sister and I weren't raised together, and I was the only grandchild for a while, she was the closest thing to a sibling that I had and now she's my very best friend.

Most importantly, my grandmother introduced me to Jesus. While she was already saved, my grandfather gave his life to the Lord later than my grandmother did. Being raised by my grandparents meant that I was often in church. If you ask her, she will tell you that I was saved at the young age of three. Of course, I didn't know what being saved fully meant until later, but it set the foundation. She taught me the importance of tithing, that "I can do all things through Christ that gives me strength", and that "Obedience is better than to sacrifice " - although that's a lesson that I had to learn the hard way. As I've gotten older, I've grown to build a relationship with God for myself and it has carried me through this journey.

Growing up, my grandmother wasn't rigid or extra controlling. While I was in church every time the doors opened, she gave me some freedom. I could go to parties, but I couldn't sleep over with friends. She knew what could happen if she did not give me boundaries. I was aware not to sit on men's laps or be alone with men without a female present. I also knew not to talk back, and I knew that if she asked me to do something, she wasn't going to ask twice. I loved school and hated to miss a day. I loved it so much I became a teacher. While in school, my grandmother didn't play about grades or behavior. She was a firm believer in "spare the rod, spoil the child." I tried my best not to test that out. When I started dating, my boyfriend could visit, but I knew what not to do. I didn't even try. Sneaking out never even crossed my mind.

As an adult, my fiancé could sleep over, but we had to sleep in separate rooms. I refused to have sex before I was married, because I was afraid that God was going to make an example out of me. All it takes is one time and to me it wasn't worth the risk. My mom and my sister had their children young, and some of my other family members had also become teenage mothers. I didn't want that to be my story. Even though I wanted to be a mother, I knew that I would have to be married before that happened. To me it seemed as though teenage pregnancy ran in my family, and I would rather eat a jean jacket than tell my grandmother at any other age than grown that I was pregnant. She'd always say, "I'm not raising any more babies.", and often her words - "if you bring a baby in here, where you goeth, your baby goeth" played in the back of my mind. I know if it came down to it she would help, but I didn't want to find out.

Omesha G.

# CHAPTER TWO

The concept of happily ever after was never lost on me. I was always drawn to babies. Whenever there was a new baby in the family, I couldn't wait to hold them. When other kids sat in deep conversation with their imaginary friends, I was planning a life for my imaginary children, two beautiful brown girls and a handsome little boy. I don't recall exactly what they looked like, but they were my kids, so I know they were beautiful and brown. Whatever fairytales their minds could concoct, mine were made up of living beings I could hold. I dreamt of them as I went to the grocery store with Goshiki, Gobagain, and Gogate in tow. "Come on before y'all get left." I recall telling them as I was leaving the store with my grandmother. I laugh every time I say their names but, they were my children until having my own became a reality.

When I grew older and they faded into my distant memories, I would take a sheet of paper from my notebook and create a list of new names for my future children. The names were creative, usually a blend of friends and family member's names. I had the first and middle name, all I needed was the last name which would be the last name of who I would marry, or whatever the last name was of the boy I was dating at the time. Boyfriends were far and few between, so the last name was more often than not left blank.

Not only did I plan the names of my children, but I would often plan out my future wedding details as well. I wanted children, but I also wanted to be a wife and I knew one needed to happen for me in order for the other to happen. I'd write down what color I wanted my wedding to be and who I wanted my bridesmaids to be. I recall getting paper out during down-time in class and playing M.A.S.H. with my peers. It's a game to "predict" who you'd marry, what kind of job you'd have, what kind of car you'd have and how many children you'd have from the options you'd write down on the paper. Making up names for my future children was a fun and innocent activity. My dreams of motherhood were real. My dreams of one day becoming a wife were real. I held them with the same intent that my classmates held their dreams of becoming a doctor, lawyer, nurse, or firefighter.

It never occurred to me that someone could find fault in my dreaming. When I was in the fifth grade, I sat quietly in my afterschool program making a list of potential baby names. The after school teacher walked by, saw what I was doing and took my paper. I remember them fussing at me, but I did not understand the problem. I wasn't perfect, of course, but I tried my best to stay out of trouble. I was an honor roll student, remembering my grandmother didn't play about those grades. Now I was being punished for making up names for my future children. Was I actually punished? No, but taking the paper felt like a punishment. I didn't get the paper back, and now I have to try to remember the names I'd already written down or come up with new ones.

So, writing is my preferred form of communication. When I needed to have difficult conversations, I would write a letter. It was a Thursday. I remember because I usually rode the bus, but my grandmother would take me to school on Thursdays. This particular Thursday, instead of going straight to my class, I stopped in the hall to talk to my cousin. Time slipped away from me, and I realized I was about to be late for class. I couldn't afford to be tardy, because if I got another one that would mean in-school suspension which was run by a friend of my grandmother. I ran down the hall with my destination in mind, blocking out those around me.

Apparently, I didn't hear the teachers that I ran past asking me to stop running, so they followed me to class to tell my teacher. So now, not only am I late, but I'm also in trouble for running down the hall and being unintentionally insubordinate. My worst fear had come to life, I got a write up which meant the following day I had in- school suspension.

I already knew what that meant when my grandmother found out. Here comes the rod! A switch was her rod of choice. Well, I had a plan. I decided to write my grandmother a letter telling her that I was too old for spankings now and if she would consider grounding me instead. I came home from after school and stalled for 10 minutes by walking a few laps around the house. My great uncle was outside making it no better, teasing me saying, "Oh you bout to get it." I was stressed. I finally got the courage to go inside and place the letter I'd written on the table. The letter was never read, I did not get grounded, and I still got a spanking, because "How you gon' learn in ISS." Even though it was only for one class period and not the entire day. It was worth a try. But I never got in school suspension again.

Being that writing was my preferred way of communication it would make sense that I would also use my pen to record my dreams. I was often misunderstood. I got in trouble often, but I wasn't doing what some of my peers were doing. It wasn't unusual for me to do or say something out of naivete–not understanding the negative connotations, but I was a child, and I did as children do. I wasn't very popular with the boys, nor did I try to rush myself to adulthood. I just had my lists.

I had my lists and my desire to be a wife, but was I confident that it would happen for me?

No. I worried that I may not get married. I mean, I wasn't the most popular with the guys at all when I was in school. They didn't look my way. I didn't have the big booty and wasn't necessarily pretty to them. I recall the boys rating the girls in our grade on a scale of 1-10. My rating was always low. Talk about a hit to my self-esteem. For a while, I wasn't pretty to myself. I hated what I saw when I looked in the mirror and would question why God made me this way. Yes, my grandmother affirmed me but that wasn't enough. I allowed how others saw me to affect how I saw myself.

Although I wasn't very popular among the guys, if I liked someone I'd shoot my shot with them often being turned down. That wasn't very popular back in the day and was viewed as desperate. Even still, who I would marry and would I ever be married was always a thought in the back of my mind. So, I never really dated for fun. Every person I dated I wondered if they would be the one that would be my husband. Creating a future for us in the confines of my imagination. If I'm honest my standard wasn't very high. If they liked me, I would like them.

When I got to my senior year in high school and began to think of what college I would go to, I decided that I would go to a Christian college so that I could meet my Christian husband. I ended up going to a public college, The University of North Carolina at Greensboro. Although I did not go to a Christian college, I still had hopes that I would meet my Christian husband in college.

It was always my goal to wait until I was married to have sex. Yes, I did sexual things with guys before I was married. I wasn't 100 percent innocent and pure, but we never went all the way. You would think that it would be easy to abstain while dating a fellow Christian, but we all know that's not always the case. I get it, our flesh will get to acting all the way up. I know mine does.

The bible says,

"I find then a law, that, when I would do good, evil is present with me."

- Romans 7:21(KJV)

So even when trying to do things the way God designed for us to do them, our flesh will definitely trip us up. That's why it was and still is important for me to be with someone who also has the desire to abstain from sex before marriage.

My husband and I waited until we were married to have sex. After our marriage ended and I began dating again, waiting again stopped being the goal, which went against my conviction. Sometimes, I even stopped feeling convicted for a little bit. During that time, I learned that no matter how far we feel like we have gone, God is right there waiting for us to get back on track and come to him. He is there to listen. I had to be honest with God at one point and tell him, "God, Ima need you to take the taste out of my mouth. I know you are not pleased but I enjoy what I am doing. Help me!"

Even through all of that, I am glad that

"There is therefore no condemnation to them which are in Christ Jesus, who walk not after the flesh, but after the Spirit."

- Romans 8:1(KJV)

Omesha G.

# CHAPTER THREE

Looking back at my dating history, almost every guy that I dated, I had to beg to make a commitment. I had no security in what we had. We stayed in what seemed like the "talking stage." After some time, I would ask them something like "so what are we doing?" Or I'd ask them in some way about us being more about what we were. It definitely felt too much like begging.

My high school boyfriend and I "talked" for a while until I asked him to make it official. He kept making excuses until he finally asked me to be his girlfriend, but I'm certain it was more because I kept asking and not because he really wanted to. At least not initially. The same thing happened with a guy I dated long distance. We were basically in a situationship. We finally became official, because I kept asking him. He asked me to be his girlfriend through a letter, but the relationship didn't last long. With each guy, even after we broke up, I still kept them around and it went back to being a situationship because something was better than nothing, right?

I even tried dating websites both before and after marriage. The last guy that I dated before my husband I had really hoped was the one, but it didn't take much for my mind to go there. He was a nice guy, and he was a Christian. That was enough for me. Then one day he told me that basically God told him I wasn't the one. Those words single-handedly set ablaze the future with him that I had created in my imagination.

I didn't just move on from him and continue to wait for the one that God did have for me. I still stayed connected to him for a little while and ended up in yet another situationship. The elusive one that I have been searching for felt so far from my reality. I felt as though if I wasn't waiting for a commitment from a guy, then I didn't have many options. Men didn't seem to notice me.

It wasn't until I met my husband that I found someone who was sure about wanting to be with me without me having to ask them. He knew what he wanted, and he knew quickly. I liked that.

One day as I was scrolling on Instagram, I received a direct message. It was from the man that I would go on to marry. The message said something along the lines of him wanting to get to know me, and he included a picture of himself. I was less than intrigued, because I didn't find him attractive. So, I told him that I was focusing on school. He was understanding, but I was disappointed. Getting presented with options you don't like while waiting on your spouse can feel like "God is playing in your face", if I'm being honest. Of course, I told my friends about the message. Soon after, I was at dinner with two friends, and they convinced me to give him a chance. Although I wasn't attracted to him, he had a nice personality. They encouraged me to look past the physical. Later that evening my friend took my phone and responded to him on my behalf. After a few exchanges I took my phone back and continued the conversation. He was nice, Christian, and checked off a few boxes on my list. Maybe it's worth a shot and maybe he would be more attractive to me in person.

When we met, unfortunately I did not find him more attractive in person. We met at a restaurant in downtown Greensboro called Dame's Chicken and Waffles. We didn't talk as much as two people who were trying to get to know each other would, but he did make me laugh. He discovered my favorite candy through my Instagram and brought it to my car at the end of the evening. I wasn't trying to impress him initially, so I didn't put much into what I wore that night. I wore a pair of jeans from JCPenney, a brown and cream colored striped polo shirt, with brown polo high top shoes to match and a brown knitted hat. I was comfortable. After we started dating he'd talk about how I was dressed that night, but it didn't stop him from pursuing me. Although I wasn't attracted to him initially, he won me over. Maybe it was the fact that I finally had someone interested in, and actively pursuing me. We continued to talk for a week, then we had our first official date.

He laid it on thick on the first date and was very thoughtful. He lived about 30 minutes from me, and decided he would come to pick me up. We went to a restaurant near where he lived. I don't recall the name of the restaurant, but it was elegant with a rooftop. When we arrived, there were roses and my favorite candy waiting for me. It was encouraging. I had never had anyone do something like this for me. We attempted to sit on the rooftop, but we were chased inside by the chill in the air. After getting to know him better, I realized I had put too much emphasis on the physical. Though I did not find him attractive, it was nice to have somebody. I didn't want to miss a great chance at love. After only a week of getting to know each other he asked me to be his girlfriend.

People around me during that time tried to tell me that we were moving too quickly, and a week was too soon for us to make it official, but I didn't want to hear it. My response was, "The heart wants what the heart wants." but we all know the heart can be deceptive. I just had to "see for myself."

Omesha G.

# CHAPTER FOUR

When we first started dating, I was still in college and lived in one of the apartments on campus. He would come by to visit me. One particular night he came by and my roommate who was also one of my close friends started asking him questions like friends do. She asked him what he liked about me, and he said that he liked the fact that I was conservative. My friend said, "She's really not." And she was right. I am not conservative at all, but as two people in our early twenties, that wasn't something that made us reconsider things. In hindsight, it should've been a sign that we probably weren't nearly as compatible as we thought we were. It was something that caused us to bump heads a lot in our relationship and even more in our marriage.

I know you may be thinking, "Why did you even date him?" "Did you like him at all?" and I'll answer that with - it wasn't all bad at first. Once I got past the physical, which didn't really take long, I really started to like him.. He was funny and I enjoyed his company. I used to enjoy spending time with him. I would look forward to him coming over on Thursdays and spending the weekend with me. I would hate it when it was time for him to leave and would try to convince him to stay. In the beginning he was really kind and considerate. I believe that he still was underneath all the other things that showed on the surface.

He told me he loved me pretty soon after we started dating, and I said it back. I told one of my close friends, and she said "but you didn't mean it, did you?" I didn't. But taking it back was harder once I said it. I don't think I ever really did. Again, multiple people in my life, at that time, thought we were moving too quickly, but I wasn't trying to hear what they were saying. I can't blame him for that.

At the end of my senior year, I got my first apartment, and he bought me things for my apartment. One time I went out of town and when I came back he had bought me a bunch of new clothes, shoes and jewelry. Gift giving was his love language. So, his gifts were pretty thoughtful and well planned out. So, again, it didn't start out badly and even as the relationship progressed there were good moments. However, the good didn't outweigh the bad.

I recall watching Tyler Perry's "Why Did I Get Married" and Patricia told the girls to write a list of the good and the bad, and if the good outweighed the bad, then they should fight for their marriage. At this point in my own relationship, there had begun to be trouble in paradise, and I thought maybe I should try Patricia's idea. If I'm completely honest, and I wasn't, the good did not outweigh the bad. That was yet another sign that we probably should go our separate ways. We weren't even married yet, not even a full year into our relationship and I'm making this list. Huge Red flag!

I didn't see the red flags until we were about a month or so into our relationship. It was the day after graduation, and I needed to run to the store. I still had my bonnet on, and he didn't like it. He freely shared his distaste for my public image. "You don't care about your appearance," he would say. I did care, just not in the way he wanted me to. I knew that no one could be picture-perfect at all hours of the day or night. If my nail polish is chipped, it could wait until I have time to fix it. He tried to make me into the version of a wife he wanted. He thought I was "her" based off of a few pictures on Instagram, but we know that Instagram is a highlight reel where you post the best. Who is "her"? You ask. She's "the always put together" church girly, girl. The girl that is super feminine. She wore makeup and heels more often than not and kept her hair and nails done. He wanted more of a Regine, and I was more of a Khadijah. He gave me an example of who he wished I was more like. It was someone we both knew and went to church with at the time. Yeah, I was nothing like her.

What he saw wasn't all that I was. He didn't like it when I wore my Timberland boots or tennis shoes. I recall one day at work, I was standing outside with my coworker. She was working the car rider line. She yelled at a student not to run out so she wouldn't get hit because the cars were moving. The parent of that scholar complained about the teacher yelling but the parent assumed it was I that yelled. The parent was white and so was my coworker. Her assumption rubbed me the wrong way, because it wasn't me, but she assumed it was. It just had to be the Black teacher that did it. Maybe that was a reach, but that's how I felt. Well later that evening my husband and I went out to eat dinner. At dinner I told him what happened, thinking he would be on my side. That day I had on jeans, a sweater and my timberland boots. When I told my husband what happened he said "Did you have that on? I would've thought it was you too." He wanted me to look feminine and dainty, but I wear a size twelve. My shoes could never be dainty. He had an opinion about the way I dressed or styled my hair. Getting dressed was never just getting dressed. I had to think about what he would say. "Will he like this?" or "He probably won't like this." We had disagreements on my appearance more often than not. It was tiring but he got what he wanted because many times I wore things that I didn't like. Over time, my wardrobe for the most part became things that he liked to see me in, and I learned to like it although it wasn't really my style. It was a challenging and exhausting time, feeling like who you are isn't good enough. If there were ever two people who shouldn't be together, we were them.

Overtime things started to shift but overall, we didn't have an emotional connection. I became more attracted to him physically, but I didn't like him as a person. He didn't like my appearance. I stopped wanting to be around him. It was just my new normal. The signs were all there. To be fair, I tried. I tried hard to love him or even like him. Since our families were so well connected and got along, I felt obligated to go with the flow. I didn't know how to leave. The things that we seemed to have in common were quickly drowned out by so much negativity and toxicity.

In our early stage of dating, I told him that I wanted to wait till we were married to have sex, but one day, I turned around to find him naked. He began to curse more frequently and spoke to me in detestable ways. I tried to push those things to the back of my mind. Before I knew it two years had gone by, and a proposal was on the horizon.

I hoped that he would be nicer being that we'd be getting married soon and spending the rest of our lives together. I knew that a proposal was on the horizon because we talked about marriage early on. We had a date picked, I was just waiting on a proposal. We were on the same page in wanting to be married, we just shouldn't have married each other. My goal remained. I was determined to be married by 25 and have two kids by 30. What happens when you get everything you asked for, but not in the way you want it?

Before I started dating him, I already had a fear of marrying the wrong person. As a Christian, divorce is usually frowned upon. So, for me, it wasn't an option. While we were dating, I fasted for three days so that I could be sure that God wanted me to marry this person.

During the same time, I went to a concert with one of my good friends and had a great time. After the concert, I posted a picture on Facebook with the caption "The only thing I'm missing is him." The next day while I'm at work, I received an unexpected message from a young lady I went to college with. We were both in the Neo Black Society on campus as well as Facebook friends. She saw the post I put up after the concert, which made her reach out to me. Apparently, around that same time my boyfriend and future husband had DM'd her attempting to shoot his shot. He told her he wanted to get to know her. He had also messaged her friend, too. Pretty much saying the same thing he said to me when he DM'd me. He had told her that we weren't together anymore. When she reached out to me and showed me the proof in the form of screenshots, I was deeply hurt. To me, this was cheating, and I had never, to my knowledge, been cheated on before. It felt like a slap in the face, because I am here giving him a chance while looking past things that I don't like about him, and he betrays my trust?

I showed him the message, and he apologized, asking me to give him another chance. I had to think about it, because I wasn't sure if I wanted to. That weekend, we had a wedding to attend, and we were also supposed to go back home to my hometown to visit. In spite of everything that transpired, I still put his desires as well as my own ego in front of the voice of God.

During this time, I leaned on my friends' advice. I shared with them about what was going on, and then I talked with him, and his response was "Don't let what your friends say make you miss out on this relationship." Somehow, this persuaded me. I decided to give him another chance, and, yet, I never had complete peace. There was always a feeling in the back of my mind that I had disobeyed God.

If someone would have told me to leave him, I would have, but it had to be those exact words. Although I felt as though God had given me the answer to my prayer I still struggled to find my own resolve. So, I reached out to a minister that I knew, asking her to pray for me in regard to the situation, and she did. When she reached back out to me, she said "I heard God say you have all the signs you need. Try your heart." That was not what I wanted to hear. I wanted the response to be something like "God said 'he isn't the one'", but we all know we can't dictate how God does things. He had already provided me with the answer to a question I kept asking. I just had to be honest with myself. To add to my confusion my boyfriend told me that God had shown him I was the one, but God hadn't shown me that at all.

Although I wanted the response to be more plain, deep down, I knew what it meant. I had such a nagging feeling that I couldn't ignore it, but I had resolved to try my best and make things work. I knew this couldn't be my promised land. It couldn't be all of what God had for me. God isn't a God of confusion. I know now that what he has for you will come naturally and it won't be forced. There will be peace in the promise.

The message from the minister led to my first attempt to break up with him. It was about six months into the relationship. The nagging feeling I had in my heart that we shouldn't be together wouldn't let me rest. I didn't have the guts to tell him to his face, so I sent him a message saying that I didn't want to be with him anymore. With writing being my preferred way of communication, I wrote out what I couldn't say. Was it the best way? No, but it was the way that I felt comfortable expressing myself. We ended up still talking about it and he pulled at my heart strings with his tears, a performance that persuaded me to stay with him. Later that evening we went to dinner, we took pictures and we posted them on Facebook as if nothing was even wrong. The second attempt was about four months after that. It was February, after valentines day. I sent him a message on my way to work. A few hours later I got a message that my Papa had passed away. A break up and a death? You can only imagine the distress I was going through at work. The attempt to breakup was unsuccessful. He used my Papa's passing to his advantage saying people were going to wonder why he wasn't there at the funeral. Thanks to my ego I was convinced and against my better judgment I stayed once again.

Truth is, I dreaded starting over. My desire to be

married was stronger than anything else. We knew that we were eventually getting married. We even knew the date already. All that was left was the proposal. We looked at rings multiple times and I knew exactly what ring he wanted. It was a silver band with diamonds around it. So, at the mall, I went to the jewelry store and bought the ring, on impulse. There was no doubt in my mind that my ring was coming. Most of my doubts surrounded whether we should be married, but I knew he wanted to marry me. As an act of faith, I bought his ring as a way of sealing my own commitment to marriage. My thought process was that if I bought his ring, then I would have to go through with it. The ever present nagging feeling in the back of my mind took up residence, but I still ignored it. I thought maybe if I prayed about it enough God would eventually straighten out our issues and bless our marriage. I allowed my desire to be married to be louder than God's voice and my obedience to God. I didn't trust His plan for me and tried to make it happen on my own. I truly desired Him to "bless my mess."

Soon I found myself compromising on one of the things I had written down on my treasured list - attending a good church. I loved my church and didn't want to leave. In order for us to be together, my husband would have to be a member. Knowing this, he joined the church, and eventually became a deacon. Everything looked good on the outside and even though we were in the same church, I still felt that we were unequally yoked. His actions weren't of someone that was submitted to God. It wasn't of someone that would lead our home in a Godly way outside of going to church. We attended the same church I was at when we first met about a year into our marriage.

However, he soon decided that he wanted to leave and go back to his home church. I fought this decision as hard as I could. I'd talked about it with my best friend and my grandma to see if they could get him to change his mind, but he had his mind made up and I didn't want us to worship at two different churches. Some people don't mind doing this, but that's not what I wanted. I wanted us to grow and serve together under the same ministry, so I made the sacrifice. We left together and began attending his home church. I wasn't happy with the decision at all. Talking about leaving would bring me to tears. When people would ask me why we left I didn't give details on why he wanted to leave, but I did say "he wants to go back to his home church." He didn't like that response because it seemed like I wasn't being supportive about the decision and was putting it all on him, but it was the truth. It wasn't my decision, and I didn't want to leave. I tried to make the best of it by getting involved in serving. I joined the choir and media team. I even met some really great people, one who would eventually go on to be my child's Godmother. Once we separated, I left that church. I mean, I was only there for him.

Even though it would probably make sense to go back to the church I originally attended, I felt as though God was leading me to a different ministry that I knew about. This was during the pandemic, so most churches were virtual. I am not a fan of virtual churches, but I joined that ministry anyway. I struggled to feel connected there. To be honest, I also didn't try very hard to connect with anyone there.. On top of that, I was missing my old church. Afterall, I had history there, and I had attended for 8 years before my husband decided we had to leave. So, I ended up rejoining that ministry, but it was different. I struggled because again, most churches were still virtual and so was this one. Even though I had rejoined, I remained distant and didn't get involved much.. I soon stopped watching the sermons and this led me to being just out there without a spiritual covering.

I began to feel like I had drifted from God. I wasn't acting too bad, but I was doing things that I knew weren't pleasing to him. I was losing myself in the midst of exploring my freedom and trying to find myself. One day, a friend reached out to ask if I was still a member of the church I had joined after my separation. I wasn't. I told her I didn't like virtual church and was longing to attend in person. She told me that Harvest City Church was back open and having in-person services, so I went to visit. I visited for about 2, maybe 3 weeks before I decided to join. Those few short weeks that I visited felt like a breath of fresh air. I could breathe again, and I didn't even realize that I was holding my breath. Joining this ministry was one of the best decisions I have made while on this journey. Yes, I had my friends and family, but this ministry gave me community. I didn't have to walk this journey alone. I am forever grateful for Pastor Bill Russell and my Harvest City Church family.

# CHAPTER FIVE

The time that I waited my entire life for had finally come. It was January 12th, 2017. I had a photoshoot booked to commemorate my 25th birthday. My hair was done. I had a sew- in cut into a bob. My nails were done, my makeup was done, and I had my custom skirt made by a friend. There were a few issues, but overall, everything was going according to plan. That night after the photoshoot, we had plans to go to dinner. First, we stopped by my apartment so that I could change into the shoes he bought me for my birthday.

While we were there, he proposed in our messy bedroom with a cheap ring from Walmart. He said he was testing the waters to be sure I'd say yes before he did it for real in front of all of our family and friends. We looked at rings quite a few times. He always picked out the bigger, more flashy rings, while I wanted something a little more modest. So when he proposed in our bedroom with that tiny, cheap ring from Walmart, I was a little disappointed, because, well, I expected more and he had talked a big game.

Nonetheless I said yes.

We pulled up to dinner at a Fishbone Grill. I wobbled inside wearing one the most uncomfortable pair of heels I'd probably ever worn. They were cute cheetah prints but uncomfortable, nonetheless. As I walked into the restaurant, I was in complete shock to see my friends and family there. I looked over and saw my family and my eyes instantly pooled with tears. At the time, they lived 3.5 hours away and it was a weekday, so I was wondering what they were doing there. I was still oblivious to the fact that he was about to propose for real. I thought it was just a surprise birthday dinner. As I greeted my friends and family, I started showing everybody my ring and they were less than enthusiastic and perplexed because they showed up for an engagement, which, of course, I had no idea of. After a while, my fiancé leads me to the front, he does a little speech and proposes again. I am, once again, in utter shock. Of course, I said yes. He takes the fake ring off my finger, and replaces it with a real, much bigger ring.

As much as I'd like to think that the proposal led to a blissful celebration and onto a wonderful time of planning, there was a lot under the surface that soon tainted my lifelong dream. As previously mentioned, for my birthday, I had a sew-in that was cut into a bob. Initially, my now fiancé didn't have a problem with my hair, but as time went on he began to point out things he didn't like about it. I wasn't in love with it either, but I could deal with it until I was ready to take the style down.

The day after the proposal, we took a trip to the mountains as a way of extending my birthday celebration. I wish I could say the trip was an exciting time especially after becoming newly engaged, but it wasn't. I was excited to be planning a wedding but not excited that I was about to spend the rest of my life with him. This experience taught me that marriage itself is more important than the wedding. I knew that but sometimes experience is the best teacher. Don't get me wrong you can have a beautiful wedding and a beautiful marriage. One doesn't have to come without the other, but you definitely don't want to be more prepared for the wedding than the marriage as one is only for a day, but the other is supposed to be for a lifetime.

He complained and had an attitude about my hair almost the entire trip. If he didn't like something, he didn't know how to express it and just move on. He allowed it to affect his mood until things went the way he wanted them to. I felt as though things were settled and there was nothing I could do about it at this point. Talking it out wasn't an option. To try to make the situation a bit more pleasant, I kept a hat on the majority of the trip. I knew he wouldn't be satisfied until he got his way, so the sew-in was taken down. When we got back home we stopped at his grandmother's house, and she helped me take it out. I knew otherwise he wouldn't be satisfied, and I wouldn't have any peace.

Once again, he got what he wanted.

While we were dating, all I wanted was out, but I was afraid to call it quits. I wasn't confident enough to walk away and just stand on my decision. Looking back, I realize I was desperate. Desperate for a relationship, for companionship. I recall earlier in our relationship that I had done something that made him upset and I said "I thought I was going to lose you." I cringe when I think about it. I can't believe I let those words cross my mind let alone slip off my tongue. I believe that gave him the confidence to believe that he could treat me any kind of way and I would stay because I needed him. I say this in the humblest way possible, but he actually needed me more than I needed him. There were things in our marriage that if I didn't do them they would not get done. Financially, I held us together, some things we got, it was based off of my credit such as the house and the car, even some furniture. I was the cook, I was the more educated one, helping him fill out resumes and applications. I never threw any of that in his face or made him feel less than, but it surely wasn't appreciated.

Once we were engaged, I felt even more stuck because we had already started to pay for the wedding. To stop would have resulted in a waste of our money, my dad's money and my grandparent's money. So, how could I walk away now? Not only that, but I was also afraid of his reaction if I decided to walk away at this point. I feared that he would be angry and I didn't know what his anger would lead to. More harsh words? Vandalism of my things? I didn't want to find out.

For the majority of our relationship, we lived together, we shacked up as the saints call it. So, it was also hard for me to leave because I felt he wouldn't have anywhere else to live. He told me that he couldn't go back to his mom's when he moved out. I didn't fact check, I just took his word for it. So, in my mind if we didn't work out, he wouldn't have anywhere else to go. I was putting his needs above my own.

During this time, there continued to be signs, red flags, that I should walk away. I remember a Sunday morning before church when we had stopped to get breakfast. I can't recall exactly what we had a disagreement about, but he spilled a drink in the car and ended up cursing me out for it. I felt as though I was being hit, but with words instead of his fist. We stopped at the car wash to clean the mess up and there was a man nearby that heard us. He just looked at me and shook his head in disappointment at how I was allowing my husband to treat me. At least, that's how I interpreted it. I felt as though many people didn't understand or had the ability to see things from my perspective. From the inside, looking out, I was in an unsafe, domestically abusive situation and I had no idea how I would get out. We went to church like normal and I had to put on a front like all was well. All I could do was weep in service. A friend I was sitting beside rubbed my back as I wept, not knowing the details of what happened but people didn't ask questions because they assumed I was crying in worship. In spite of all of this, we gave marriage counseling a try. I expected God to show them that we shouldn't be together, thinking maybe this can be my way out. During the counseling sessions, we discussed how he treated me.

Somehow, he ended up being the one who cried.

That made me feel hopeful that he would change. Maybe this was what was needed, but he didn't. I even told them my concerns. I told them the incident of him sending the girl a DM expressing interest in her and lying saying that we had broken up earlier on in our relationship. I explained how it happened at the conclusion of my fast, which had left me to wonder if it was a sign from God. They didn't see it as cheating and didn't even really let me explain the situation. It was kind of brushed over like I made a big deal out of nothing. I can say that I also wasn't completely honest with how I felt during our counseling sessions. Since then, I have learned that counseling won't work if you aren't completely honest, but how could I let them know what I was truly feeling? I wanted to be told straight out not to get married to him, but I didn't want it to be because of anything I said. I wanted God to show them. Rescue me!

You would think that planning a wedding would be a happy time, but it just caused more red flags to show even brighter. We got married at Castle McCulloch in Jamestown, NC. The day that we were supposed to go meet with them we drove separately. I'm not sure if we were arguing on the way to our cars, but I said something to him, not trying to be disrespectful, and all I hear is "Fuck you too."

Apparently, he thought I said it to him, but I hadn't, which caused me to be confused at his response. When

I told him that I didn't say that, he apologized, but the damage had been done. We were on our way to pay for our wedding venue and that was how he chose to speak to me.. This was not out of the norm and didn't surprise me. Not always to that extent, but I expected as much.

One thing I know for sure is that how a man treats his mom is a sign of how he will treat you. There were times when I witnessed him speak to his mom with the same disrespect. Even to the point that his mom called me one day and told me how he had cursed his dad out and had fussed her out about something in regard to the wedding. She said that if he would talk to her like then there was no telling how he is going to talk to me. Little did she know, I was already experiencing it.

# CHAPTER SIX

My husband felt more like a parent than a partner. Marriage only magnified our problems and while I hoped that things would change, they didn't get better. When we first began dating, I noticed how his attitude would change when he didn't have money. One night we met to go hang out in the city that he lived in at the time. While we were together, I noticed that his attitude was different. He was shorter than normal with me. He wasn't laughing or very talkative. I thought it was something that I had done but when I asked him what was wrong, he said nothing. Eventually, he told me what was wrong and apologized for how he acted. He told me that he gets in a bad mood when he doesn't have money. At the time, I didn't see that as a red flag. I mean, I too am guilty for allowing how much money is or is not in my bank account to alter my mood.

As time went on I learned that he was as obsessed with money as he was with my appearance. His demeanor would change when money was low, and he checked the bank accounts multiple times per day. Money dictated his attitude and altered his behavior. It could drive him to steal groceries or cash a fraudulent check. I was the opposite. I did not operate with a budget and would not plan for bills. As the main breadwinner, I was confident in my ability to contribute. Even though he found shelter in that, we would often argue because I wouldn't tell him when certain bills were due, and he didn't like to be caught by surprise. He would plan the money out to a T and if things were off, or if there was something extra that he didn't plan for that needed to be paid - he was not happy. I refused to be stressed about bills and money, or let it control me to that extent. He often mistook that as me not caring.

Whenever I would ask him what his plans were, he could only say that he wanted to make a lot of money. He didn't have a plan, a college degree, or a trade. As the main breadwinner, I tried to make sure that I didn't throw my job in his face and respect him as the head of the house. The summers were hard because schools are closed, and teachers don't receive pay. If I wasn't making the money, things would be shaky. While it was possible to survive if he was unemployed, it was really when I was out of work that he would badger me. It seemed as though the financial load was all on me, and just like this entire marriage, I was the only one hoping that things would work out.

# CHAPTER SEVEN

Once we got married that October of 2017, my husband was ready to start a family almost immediately. Although I wanted to have a baby as well, I thought we'd wait til the following year to begin trying. He didn't want to wait so I got off of birth control and we began trying the following month after getting married. It didn't happen immediately. Being able to have a baby was something that I desired and would do whatever I needed to in order to have one even though I didn't like the person I was married to. I only wanted to sleep with him when I was ovulating. Many times, sex with him felt like rape.

Yes, I know that sounds extreme, but I recall moments of just lying there while he did what he needed to do. I would wait for it to be over so I could forget about it and go about my business. It reminded me of rape scenes in movies where the victims would stop fighting their rapist and just let him have it because it was easier than fighting. That is what would play in my mind while I would have sex with my husband. I felt as though I wasn't doing it because

I actually wanted to. I was doing it to keep the peace. I was doing it because I told him yes when he asked after turning him down multiple times already that week.

Yes, he was my husband, but I believe that sex doesn't start in the bedroom. I can't speak for anyone but myself when I say that for me it starts in my mind. So, things like getting on my nerves all day or not treating me well among other things will not make my vagina respond positively regardless of whether he was hot and ready. It is also quite possible that he wanted a baby more than he wanted to be with me. As a married woman, I knew that if all was well that a baby was inevitable. My long- awaited dream would soon come to reality. As much as I wanted to be a mother, I wasn't prepared to start trying immediately. My husband was right away, though. Without much of a fight I began the journey of creating a life with him. It wasn't instant. Despite my youth and fairly good health, it took us over a year to get pregnant. By definition, I was infertile. We had been trying for over a year and were unsuccessful. It was routine. We would track my ovulation, have sex, wait two weeks and then my period would come. Then we'd do it all over again. Month after month, disappointment after disappointment when my period would show.

Then that one month came.

With period symptoms and pregnancy symptoms being so close I thought my period was coming any day now. But it never showed up. I took a pregnancy test about a week after my missed period and to our surprise it was positive. That was in March of 2019, and we announced our pregnancy on Easter a few weeks later. It seemed as though everything in life was finally looking up.

So many doors opened for us around that time. We closed on our house in January and got a new car and then our dreams of finally becoming parents came true.

That was short lived.

A few weeks after finding out that I was pregnant I was let go from my job. The timing couldn't have been any worse. Now I am pregnant with no insurance, and we just purchased a house and a new car. What are we going to do? During that time, I fell asleep at the wheel and hit a mailbox messing up the front of my car.

"What else could go wrong?" was the loudest thought that crossed my mind. I had been so excited to have finally conceived. And, yet, caution reminded us that we couldn't get too excited, because we both feared the possibility of a miscarriage.

Finding out that we are pregnant only to have so much back to back bad news was discouraging and our lives were flipped upside down. To ease our anxiety, we met with our pastor, and we told him we were expecting. He prayed over my womb and prayed over us. We felt hopeful that everything would be alright. Immediately, we began to plan a baby shower and gender reveal. We had already purchased a crib and stroller that we had bought in faith while we were waiting to conceive. We chose the names we wanted for each gender. If it were a boy his name would be Gavin Thomas and if it were a girl her name would be Hailey Camille. I wanted a little girl although I had a feeling it was a boy. They say that if you are carrying a girl you want sweet things and if you are carrying a boy you prefer savory. Well as much as I loved sweets I just couldn't stand it, but I was still keeping my fingers crossed for a girl. Unfortunately, the joy of pregnancy and planning for a gender reveal and baby shower were cut short.

I had planned on giving birth at the local birthing center. I had only seen the baby once since conception as I had lost my job very shortly after finding out I was pregnant, and my insurance ended almost immediately. I applied for Medicaid and being that I was pregnant I was approved. We were set to see the gender of the baby in a few short weeks.

In the last week of June, our church had Vacation Bible

School. The first night was on a Tuesday and I had begun feeling some discomfort. The pain lasted a couple days, but I scheduled an appointment to see my midwife that Thursday. I went to my appointment and the baby had a strong heartbeat. All seemed well and they told me the discomfort that I was feeling was just growing pains and to take some pain meds and get a heating pad. When we left the appointment we went straight to Target for a heating pad and pain meds.

However, even with the prescribed suggestions, the discomfort didn't go away. The next day, I went to work still in pain. They tried to get me to go home, but I wanted to stay. While at work I was peeing a lot which didn't seem abnormal for a pregnant person, but what was different was the amount of fluid that was coming out. The last time I went to the bathroom I heard a gush of water and immediately, I thought, "that sounds like my water broke." I dismissed the thought because I was only 16 weeks pregnant.

I was working at the child care center of my alma mater at the time and it was nap time but they were about to get up to eat their snack. I'm sitting down in front of the computer, and I get up to go make the snack for the students. As soon as I turn the corner of the other side of the bookshelf I feel something running down my leg. I thought it was water. I look down and there is so much blood. I began to yell for the teacher that I was helping. I did my student teaching under her a few years prior and we had grown really close. She was and still is like a mother figure to me. I'm so grateful that she was the one there that day. She of course knew I was pregnant, and she immediately called 911. Thankfully the students couldn't see anything because I was on the other side of the bookshelf. There was a parent there to pick up their child and she helped get the children out of the room and to the other classroom. The EMS came and helped me on the stretcher. I looked over to where I was sitting and saw what I thought was possibly my baby. I sobbed.

All I could do was cry.

I just knew that my worst fear had come to reality and that I had just lost my baby. Thankfully, my job wasn't too far from the Women's Hospital. The teacher I was working with called my husband and he met me there. Once they checked me in I got out of my blood soaked clothes. I remember, it was a red white and blue striped summer dress and tan flip flops. The hospital gown became my new covering. As much as it could. A nurse came in and checked the baby's heart rate to ease my mind and the heart beat was so strong. I had hoped that the baby would be ok, but still had to have an ultrasound that would ultimately determine everything.

While waiting, I had to tell my family and the baby's Godparents what was happening. My family didn't live close to me so they couldn't come up to the hospital but one of the baby's godmothers lived close by and she came up to the hospital and sat with me that night.

I waited in the room for a bit and after some time had passed they wheeled me back for an ultrasound. If you have ever had an ultrasound then you know the ultrasound techs keep a straight face and can't tell you anything, good or bad. After the ultrasound, I'm taken back to the room to wait for my midwife to come in and tell me what was seen on the ultrasound. Between the ultrasound and waiting for my midwife, I remained hopeful because the heartbeat was so strong, and I had heard stories of people bleeding but nothing being wrong with their baby.

Maybe that would be my story too and this would all be a testimony. After what seemed like eternity my midwife came in and delivered the worst news. My water broke and there was no more amniotic fluid in my sac. She told me that the baby was healthy, but it couldn't survive without any amniotic fluid. My worst fear had come to life.

Why me? Why now?

We were already going through so much.

Initially I was supposed to have a D and C which is a "dilation and curettage". That is a procedure where they go in and take the fetus out. I was terrified of what would happen next. I wasn't prepared to give birth. I wanted this to be over and for them to do whatever they needed to do and do it quickly. I didn't even want to see the baby, but as things progressed, God had begun to change my heart. I still had a little slither of hope that God would change this situation around and that my baby would be a miracle so I opted out of the D&C to give us more time, in hopes that things would turn around. I was in my room when one of the nurses came in and I expressed how I was feeling to her. I told her that I no longer wanted to do a D&C. She left and when she returned she told me that legally they couldn't do the D&C if I didn't want to, because it would technically be an abortion being as though the baby still had a heartbeat. Instead, we induced my labor so that he could be born naturally.

I prayed and cried.

I even remember "Miracle Worker" by J.J Hairston coming on. That gave me even more hope. Every time the nurse would come and check the heartbeat it was still strong. They wouldn't perform the D&C as long as the baby still had a heartbeat. The next day, the baby's heartbeat had finally stopped.

There was no more hope.

I labored that entire day and delivered Gavin Thomas the next morning. Our baby was gone before we could even celebrate. Before I could even experience what it felt like to have a baby bump or feel his little kicks inside. It was a catastrophic thing to carry and lose life within the same vessel. Going through the agony of labor with no reward.

Not many people knew, not even three of my closest friends, and certainly hadn't posted it on social media yet. I deleted the event on Facebook for my gender reveal which concerned one of my close friends. She called asking if everything was okay because she had seen that I had deleted the event. I told her what was going on, which is how my three close friends found out. She and my other close friend asked if they could come to the hospital, and I told them yes.

When I told my husband that they were coming he got upset. He was angry that I told them what was going on. I didn't understand why. Afterall, they were two of my closest friends. He didn't understand that I needed my community during such a hard time. During my stay in the hospital, every time the midwife needed to talk to us, my husband was nowhere to be found. The midwife noticed and made a comment saying something along the lines of "he doesn't know how to take care of you." I told him what she said hoping it would make him do better, but it only made him mad and made him dislike the midwife. There were two midwives that we were working with so after that he didn't want to deal with her and only wanted the other midwife.

After I was discharged from the hospital we went to my grandparent's house for about a week. Being at home and around my family always made everything better. I knew that if I could just get home to my grandparent's house that everything would be ok, even if it was just temporary.

Once we got home, we began unloading the car. Instead of assisting me, he had me carry my own bags. I carried them upstairs to our room. I think back now and wish I had just left them downstairs in the living room.

By this time, I was upset because I was still recovering from delivering my 16 week old baby. Even though the bleeding had stopped, I was still in pain. After I carried the bags upstairs, I went to the bathroom and noticed that I had started to bleed again, which happened because I had just carried luggage upstairs. I showed him that I had begun to bleed again, and, out of annoyance, said, "this is why I shouldn't be carrying bags." When he saw that it made me start to bleed, suddenly, a lightbulb came on and he understood.

Omesha G.

# CHAPTER EIGHT

Losing the baby, we tried so long for crushed us, but we didn't give up. Against better judgment, and clearance from my midwife, we began attempting to try to conceive again. I began taking pills called Clomid to increase my ovulation and it was a success.

I was pregnant again!

I went to see my midwife so that they could confirm and check my HCG levels. My levels were high enough to confirm pregnancy. A few days later, I go to the bathroom and when I wipe I see blood. I'm hopeful that the blood doesn't mean what it could mean. I scheduled an appointment with my midwife to check my levels once again, but this time the levels had gone down and indicated miscarriage. I hadn't told anyone but a few close friends that we were pregnant this time. Not even my parents or my grandparents knew. Many people didn't know until way later that I had miscarried again.

I didn't understand.

At that time, it was so hard for me to understand

why I had to go through the loss of two babies that I so badly wanted. After becoming pregnant the second time, I remember thinking "If I lose this baby too, I'll still go to church but I'm sitting in the back." As much as I wanted to be upset with God and lose faith, something in me just wouldn't let it happen. I held on to hope for the future as much as I could.

Although it hurt, I now understand a little bit more than I did before. I learned that we only see what's in front of us, but God sees the whole picture. There is purpose even in our pain. While God doesn't want to see us hurting, He uses it to bring us to where we need to be. He uses even the hard and hurtful things to bring him glory. My pastor taught us that God starts at the end and works back to the beginning. He sees everything that is happening before it gets to us. With that being said, God knew that my marriage would soon end. He also knew that my husband would unexpectedly pass away leaving me as a single parent and leaving my child(ren) without a father. I had no idea what was to come, but God did. So, although it hurt at the time and I still wonder what my children would be like, I now understand why God allowed it to happen.

With two miscarriages in the same year, we didn't give up.

We kept trying.

I kept tracking my cycles to see when I would be most fertile. He tracked my cycles as well. It was important for my husband and I to have sex whenever I was ovulating. One of those times, I was sick with a fever. I began feeling sick at church. I was disappointed to be feeling so badly because I knew that it was important for us to attempt to conceive that day but with a 100 degree fever I just wasn't up to it. I hoped that he would understand, but unfortunately he didn't. Instead, he got mad at me. I was laying down scrolling social media on my phone, which made him even more upset because if I'm sick why am I on my phone? I thought that he would understand that it took more energy to have sex than it did for me to be on my phone. I thought that he'd care that I was sick, but he was more focused on conceiving a child than my health at that moment.

Another example of his inconsideration of my well-being is that it wasn't unusual for me to get yeast infections and I couldn't figure out why. We discovered that it was because he was diabetic. He was diabetic and he refused to care for himself properly to keep the diabetes under control which in turn would leave me with yeast infections after we were intimate. There were times that I would push through the pain because it was ovulation time, but my sacrifices were not enough.

After the miscarriages, I tried to find myself. I was growing, but anything that took my time away made him jealous. He bought me a Cricut machine to do arts and crafts, but he soon regretted the purchase because it took time away from him. When I started a journaling challenge, he resented it. He felt as though he was entitled to the contents of my journal. I was trying to find a way to heal, but he wanted my attention even if there was no conversation or interaction. A lot of things felt forced, it didn't just flow. Many times, we would be on a long drive and not say a word. I had nothing to say though. I would rack my brain to think of things to talk about, but the conversations never lasted long. I'd ask a question to have a conversation and he'd answer it with a short answer. He didn't put in much effort to keep the conversation or even really initiate conversation although he was the one that would complain that we didn't talk. Deep down I believe he knew I didn't love him or want to be with him anymore. The longer we stayed together, the harder it was to hide it.

In marriage, I kept things to myself. Since I was committed to my vows, there was no need for anyone else to know the ugly details. I did not tell them that he was verbally abusive. I justified his behavior, because at least he didn't hit me. He would pinch me and then act as if he was playing. He tried to mask the abuse, but he knew that he was hurting me. To be honest, I didn't realize that him pinching me was abuse until way later, but I knew I didn't like it. He would always go just a little too hard when we were in play. He would use his strength against me. I had the bruises to prove it.

One day, he and I went to eat with one of my close friends. She saw the bruise on my arm, and I told her it came from him pinching me. Her response was, "Alright now." I think it was at that moment that he realized that what he was doing wasn't okay because he stopped doing it after that. He would fuss at me when I needed help with the trash or a flat tire so when things happened I was hesitant to call him for help. He should've been the person that I ran to for help, but I never knew how he'd react. I always felt as though I was walking on eggshells, trying not to upset him. He made me feel like I was dumb or beneath him.. He'd often compare us, describing me as having book smarts while he painted himself as the one who had the common sense or street smarts. If we were going somewhere and I was driving, he never liked it when I would use my GPS. It was as though he expected me to automatically know how to get around town, but it was normal for me to use my

GPS for everything as it has been for over ten years in the city I've called home.

To be honest, I like to say that I am directionally challenged. If I was driving there were times where he'd get mad and start to fuss because I wouldn't know where to go. I especially disliked driving downtown. I would think - if only he had let me use my GPS or at least tell me where to go. I was more willing to adjust or compromise than him. More often than not, I would let him have his way to keep the peace. Whether it was our child's name, the house we bought, wedding colors, or the theme, his preference dictated the outcome. Majority of that time I would only have sex with him so he wouldn't be mad. Sex felt like a chore more than something I enjoyed to have a deeper connection with my spouse.

There were a lot of discussions about what I would do wrong. I know we shouldn't do this, but I would tell him what he did wrong as well. We would do it to each other, to be honest. Instead of taking accountability, we pointed the finger at each other. When I would talk to him about how he'd talk to me or his language, there was always an excuse. He didn't see anything wrong with it. Sometimes I would cry hoping he'd feel bad for how he talked to me. Yes, I know that was manipulation, but I wanted him to care about how he made me feel. Sometimes, he'd blame me for how he treated me, and he would say things like "you do xyz, that's why you get treated like that." or "you must like when I talk to you like this" when I would do something he didn't like, or thought wasn't the smartest thing to do.

I often felt dumb, like I couldn't do anything right. Again, I didn't do everything right as a wife. I didn't cook, clean, or say yes to sex as often as he thought I should but none of that justified how I was treated. I didn't deserve it. I wasn't spoken to like someone he loved. He talked to me like a nigga off the street. I expressed that to him as well as our Pastor at the time when we went for counseling during our marriage. I recently went to see The Color Purple and I could relate to Celie so much. Doing all the housework. The cooking and cleaning that did get done but more often than not met with complaints instead of thanks. Having sex just to please him. He didn't make me feel ugly. But I definitely didn't feel like I was good enough. Thinking back my husband was a mild version of Mr.

There were times that I would say something alluding to me wanting to leave and he would accuse me of taking the easy way out. Although I kept most of what I felt to myself there was a friend that I would vent to near the end of our marriage. I recall telling her that I hated being married to him. She advised me to talk to someone, but I wasn't ready to confront what I was feeling yet so I brushed it under the rug and moved on yet again.

He said he loved me, but I didn't feel loved.

His actions dictated quite the opposite.

# CHAPTER NINE

By this time, I had suffered two miscarriages and was in a miserable marriage. I wasn't suicidal. I just felt stuck. I wanted more. My husband asked me one day, "Are you depressed?" Maybe I was, but what I do know is that I hated the life I was living. I wanted to find a way out that did not involve divorce. I wasn't going to kill him. I would never do that. I just desperately needed an escape. I thought about how my life would be without him. I wanted another chance to do it the right way. I had seen what a happy marriage could be, and I wanted to experience that for myself. I wanted to experience what it was like to be loved in word and in deed.

We put on a good front.

Many people thought all was well from the outside looking in but as the saying goes "everything that glitters isn't gold." What you may see on the internet is just a "highlight reel" and you never know what people are going through behind closed doors. There were people that looked up to us as a Christian Couple, so they were very shocked when they learned of our separation. I even had someone reach out to me saying that basically because we were "in the church" they thought we had it all together. That goes to show you that being a Christian doesn't disqualify you from trials and tribulations. But when you have a relationship with God you are more equipped to handle the trials because God is with you.

While I was married, I would be asked questions like "When did you know he was the one?" Or, "What do you love about him?" I hated those questions, because, to be honest, I didn't have an answer. I would always pull something out of my behind to appease their curiosity. I would say, "There wasn't one specific moment that I knew. It was a culmination of things." When in reality, I knew he wasn't the one.

In the spring of 2020, we decided to go walking downtown. It was the beginning of the pandemic, but everything wasn't shut down just yet. As usual, I wanted to be comfortable, so I wore some jeans, one of my favorite t-shirts and a pair of sneakers. What he decided to wear was more business casual, which was his usual style. When my husband saw what I had on, he didn't like it, which wasn't uncommon. He wanted me to be dressier. However, I wouldn't change my clothes. I was comfortable. I mean we were just going downtown for a walk. As a result, he had an attitude. This led to a not so fun evening.

As we were walking around, we began to argue, and he said something along the lines of "I can't do this anymore." For once, we were on the same page. That was the night when I seriously began to consider divorce. Little did he know I had left long before that. Mentally, I had been gone for a while. This was the initial time that I truly considered divorce. When I expressed that I wanted to leave, his first reaction was anger. Over and over again, he asked, "why?" and tried to toss the chair with me in it, which knocked my cup out of my hand. He later apologized and said "you shouldn't have to be afraid of a person who is supposed to protect you." When I decided that I was done, or so I thought, I left that weekend and stayed with my best friend. I didn't tell him where I was going or when I'd be back. He didn't appreciate that, but I needed to get away. I needed time to think and clear my mind.

By this point, I had reached the revelation that there didn't need to be words spoken. Enough had been said. It was time that we took a step back from each other. I told him to give me a few days so that I could think and pray about my decision. While I was gone, I confided in my best friend and, of course, she was on my side. I even talked to a few other of my close friends to ask for their prayers, but I was careful not to disclose all of the details until I was absolutely sure that I was done with my marriage. One of them said that she knew it was coming and God had revealed to her that our marriage was going to end. My friends really were my sounding boards during that time. They listened and were sympathetic as good friends are supposed to be. Along with their prayers, they helped me get through this difficult time so that I would not feel alone. Who you are connected to during challenging seasons of your life is extremely important.

So, I had told him that I would pray on my decision to stay or not. He told someone close to us at the time what was going on and they reached out to me. They asked me if I thought he was worth fighting for. I told them yes, but that was a lie. I didn't feel comfortable enough to say no. Although I wanted to leave then, I wasn't fully confident in my independence. So, I waited until I was ready to do so. In the meantime, we agreed to try to work it out.

While doing so, we met with our current Pastor, and he gave us advice on things that we could do to help our marriage. It worked for a little while, but shortly after I regretted not moving forward with my decision to leave. I felt as though I had missed my opportunity. And right along with that, my resolve to try was slipping. I felt as though I was walking around as a shell of myself. Just going through the motions existing, but not living. I didn't want to save our marriage. I wanted to be married just not to him.

Omesha G.

# CHAPTER TEN

In the beginning of summer 2020, George Floyd had been killed by police. Another unarmed Black man. There were riots and protests everywhere. My husband came home, and we began to talk about what was going on. Candace Owens had made a statement saying that she didn't support George Floyd and didn't see him as a martyr. My husband agreed with her. This was another prime example that supported my desire to be 100 percent done with my marriage. I couldn't help but to think about our black children that we would one day bring into the world and, God forbid, that something so horrific would happen to them.

Would he blame them because they didn't comply?

That opened my eyes completely.

I wanted to be able to be proud to say that this was my husband. I wanted to be able to say that I would want my son to grow up to be like his dad or for my daughter to grow up to marry someone like her dad, but I couldn't say that.

One morning, while in the shower, I remember praying something along the lines of "Lord, please let him leave me, because I don't have the guts to leave him." Not too long after that he got upset with me because I didn't want to have sex. As a result, I got the silent treatment, which was pretty usual after a disagreement. This time it went even further. I came home and he had taken all of his clothes out of the drawers in our room and put them in the guest room and left his wedding band on the dresser. I was ecstatic.

He thought it was a short-term thing, but I was done.

To me, it was an answered prayer.

To be honest, I can't say I loved him, and I don't know if he loved me. He said he did, but his actions didn't show it. I sure didn't feel loved by him. People who knew him didn't know the man I knew at home. There were two different versions of him, and one of them the world was never introduced to. He was a good guy to them. He had his good moments but the good didn't outweigh the bad. I got most of the bad.

My mind was finally made up and I told my friends that I was ready to get a divorce. I told very few people the full story, but as expected there was shock and anger towards my husband. They didn't realize how deep things had gotten over the years.. People formed their own opinions about him, and comments were made about his character. What surprised me was that, to them, all of this unfolding was simply confirmation. They had seen or sensed things that were out of order but had decided not to get involved. A decision that I respected.

When I talked to some people about what was going on and why I wanted to leave, I felt like I wasn't being heard. I felt as though people weren't listening to me. I said I wasn't happy but that wasn't the only reason I wanted to call it quits. It was way deeper than that. It at times felt as though my feelings and what I had experienced didn't matter, that I should try to save my marriage.

During that time, I was still a teacher. It was my first year teaching in public school. This was extremely different from teaching NC Pre-K at a head start program. So, in the public school world, I was a first year teacher. I was a kindergarten teacher, and my principal didn't renew my contract that year. Once again, it felt as though my life was falling apart.

But this time maybe it was falling together.

Once I decided to leave my marriage, my soon-to-be ex-husband and I went through a range of emotions. But it would be in the small details. The things that just became patterns to him that sealed my decision towards divorce. He had a habit of getting my phone and reading my text messages while we were married. Boundaries and personal space didn't exist in our marriage. If you have apple products then you know your messages that come to your phone will sync to your iPad as well. One day, I left my iPad at home.. I got a text message from him saying, "so you're talking to your friends about me? That's why I threw your tablet in the dumpster." I turned my car around so fast and flew back to my house to find him standing in the door on the phone with his mom. My friends had found his mom's page and saw a post that she shared that looked like it could've been about me and we were talking about it in the messages. My husband decided to share what we had said in private with his mom.

Looking back, I wish I'd refused to take the phone. I didn't owe him anything. And, yet, here I had found myself talking to his mom about what was said.. She denied that the post was about me and claimed that she has stayed out of what we have going on. This was the end of our conversation. I gave the phone back. After he got off the phone with his mom, that wasn't the end. He was still heated that I had talked about him with my friends. Although, facts were said, it didn't matter to him.

Here he was, fussing me out, angrily. He had worked

himself up so much that he couldn't fight the urge to fling a can of bug spray in my direction. It hit the wall, adding a dent to our decor. As stated, he said that he had thrown my iPad away, but he really hadn't. He ended up giving me my iPad back. As time went on when I talked to his mother again she said that he wouldn't talk about what happened or tell her why we were divorcing. The only thing he kept saying was "She hurt me." Upon hearing that, I was very perplexed. Out of everything I went through with him including how he talked to me and how he treated me, it was confusing to see him paint himself as the victim.

However, it made me laugh, because how did I hurt him? Was it setting boundaries and not wanting to talk to him? Or maybe it was the messages he saw of us talking about him? Regardless, it didn't compare to the things I went through. Throughout the entire process, I was encouraged to remain kind. I refrained from saying things to him about how I really felt because I can't control how people treat me, but I can control my response. That is what God will hold me accountable for.

He was angry at first and then he was sad. When we still lived together, I would hear him crying from the other room. He wanted to talk about why we were ending things. I don't think he saw what he had done as "that bad", but I refused to talk to him. I didn't want to be persuaded into changing my mind. I had finally found the courage to leave, and I didn't want anything to get in the way of that. I believe that made him angry and he felt as though I had changed from the person he was married to. "Where is the sweet Omesha?" He asked.

I hadn't changed. The sweet person he married was still there. I was the same person I just had firm boundaries and stuck with them. He tried various ways to persuade me that he had changed but there was nothing that could get me to budge on my decision. Not his friends, not my friends and not even my grandma.

All in which he talked to in order to try and get me to change my mind. By this time, I had lost my job and had a second miscarriage that my grandmother had known nothing about. He disclosed those things to her as a way to get her on his side and forced me into staying with him because he thought I needed him. My grandmother is very old school and has her views on divorce, but she wanted me to be happy. She wanted what was best for me. At first she didn't know the details. I had been protecting his character, so I didn't tell her the extent of why I was leaving. Eventually, I did tell her the full story and she still wanted what was best for me.

My grandparents were definitely a saving grace during that time especially financially. There was an SUV he bought. It was in my name because I had the better credit, but he was responsible for making the payments and paying for the insurance. Once we separated, he agreed that if he could no longer afford the payments he would give me the car back. He kept his word, but I couldn't afford the payments either. My grandparents knew that I couldn't afford the payments and walking away from my marriage left me in some debt so they took the car and the financial responsibilities of it. That's just one example of how they helped me during that time.

Now that I had made up my mind and nothing or no one could change it, my husband continued to make efforts of reconciliation in hopes of us remaining together. I honestly believed that he was hopeful all the way up until the very end. He went as far as to get advice from other married couples that we knew at church. Many people told him that they had gone through a period of separation as well during the early years of their marriage. They told him that the first few years are always the hardest. That can be true in some cases, but I didn't care about everyone else.

I told him "I don't care if Mary and Joseph went through it and worked it out. That will not be our story."

In hindsight, that probably wasn't the nicest thing to say, but that's how done I was. I was finally at peace with my decision and was going to let nothing jeopardize that. Nothing was going to come between the peace and the freedom I finally felt.

However, none of this means that the decision was easy. As time went on I believe he was able to see the damage that was done. He apologized for the way he treated me while we were together. Do I believe he'd changed? Yes, I did? I wanted him to change for himself and to be better for the next person. I just knew that he wasn't going to do that for me. Although I didn't want to be with him anymore, I did pray for him and want him to find love again, living happily ever after.

Unfortunately, he didn't get the chance.

# CHAPTER ELEVEN

In the state of NC, you have to be separated for a year before you can officially file for divorce. A year seemed so far away. I was ready to be done and completely move on.

I was ready to begin dating immediately. I didn't know that I could date while separated. Legally you can, but from a spiritual standpoint, you're still married, so it felt like it was approaching the sin of adultery. Once I found out that I could legally date during that time, I did. Was it smart to open another door before one was fully closed?

Probably not.

After marriage, I felt free. I yelled," Freedom!" from the mountaintop with my invisible bullhorn. I never came out and publicly stated that I was separated, but there were signs. I changed my name back to my maiden name on Facebook and shared certain posts that insinuated that something was going on. I had the peace that I longed for and started the journey to finding myself. In my marriage I had become the conservative person that just hadn't fit who I was. I had settled into this person that wore things that I knew he would approve of. When we separated it was my goal to wear less clothing. Not super revealing but I definitely showed more skin. I remember very soon after we separated I wore a shirt that showed my midriff a little. It was a yellow shirt. The yellow against my skin made me shine like the sun.

I felt more beautiful than I'd felt in a while and people noticed.

They knew something was different because they weren't accustomed to me showing skin in the years that I was with my husband. I learned earlier on in our relationship that showing too much skin wasn't going to fly in this relationship. One day we had planned to go hang out. I had on some dark blue skinny jeans and a pair of new balance sneakers. My shirt was a short sleeved, crop fishnet type shirt. I thought I was cute. It showed my skin. It showed some of my stomach, but it wasn't extreme. The fishnet holes were super big, and it was super revealing. Again, I thought I was cute, so I took a picture and posted it to my Instagram. I showed him the picture and he quickly let me know his distaste for my outfit saying, "You thought that was cute, didn't you?" or something to that regard. Whatever he said let me know that it wasn't going to fly in the relationship. Little did I know that was the beginning of my creative expression through what I wore being stifled. I would often get dressed thinking I was cute, and he wouldn't like it. Getting dressed wasn't just getting dressed. It came with stress. Stress about what he would think.

Before meeting him I thought I had a good sense of style and wanted to meet someone that "matched my fly" you know, complimented me. But this isn't what I had in mind.

People would complement me on what I'd have on, but it wasn't me. Oftentimes, when someone would say "I like your outfit, where did you get it from?" my response would be "I don't know, my husband got it for me." That was my response more often than not. I didn't realize how problematic that was. It was a way to control what I wore. So, I got used to dressing the way he wanted me to. As time went on I did grow to like it but again, it wasn't me.

I drew the line at church hats.

Now - that, I flat out refused.

Omesha G.

# CHAPTER TWELVE

My, now separated, husband and I lived together for months after I told him I wanted to leave, because he couldn't afford to move out on his own. This may not have been my wisest decision, but I told him not to worry about any bills pertaining to the house we shared so that he could save his money to move out. I told him I wanted a divorce in June, and he didn't move out until October.

Divorce.

It can be a touchy subject as a Christian because many don't believe in divorce. The scriptures state that divorce is acceptable due to abandonment which means the other person walked away, or because of sexual immorality. I was always fearful of marrying the wrong person because I didn't want to end up stuck in a marriage because of this exact scripture.

Well, in my case my spouse didn't abandon me and there was no sexual immorality. Was God ok with my decision? Or would I be breaking the covenant with God and ultimately committing adultery if remarried? After all I had already made a covenant with disobedience by getting married in the first place. Did I want to disappoint God again?

I prayed about it and talked to people that I trusted. In the end, I made the decision to divorce. I had made up my mind to the point where I didn't care if God approved because I had to go. I was at peace with my decision, and I believe that God was too. Yes, I was disobedient in getting married after he'd warned me not to, but I refused to believe that God wanted His daughter in a mentally, emotionally, verbally abusive marriage. I'm not telling anyone to get divorced nor am I promoting divorce.

It is my desire to see everyone's marriage to work.

Ultimately, that decision and what you choose to do is between you and God. I did what I felt was best for me.

Over the years in conversations with different people, I'd heard stories of people staying in marriages longer than they probably should have. I didn't want that to be me. I didn't want to look back over my life and be full of regret and wondering "what if". To be honest, I didn't leave just for me. I left for generations to come. I left for the children that I would eventually bring into this world. I wanted my children to be raised in a loving home and to grow up seeing their parents loving each other. It was my desire for us to be their first example of romantic love, healthy love. To leave generational wealth and legacy in the form of love. I didn't want to unintentionally teach them that love came with suffering or abuse of any kind.

I stayed away from home as much as possible. I mean who wants to live in the house with the person that they just decided to divorce but while there I tried to be as cordial as possible. We'd go get food or he'd share food with me. Him not moving out immediately was elongating the divorce process because the separation couldn't legally start until we weren't living together and I wasn't going anywhere. I mean, after all, the house was in my name, and I made more money. Once he did move out he still had a key and I'd find things missing like dryer sheets and hot sauce. This seems extreme but I'd have nightmares of him coming in while I was asleep and sexually assaulting me. I was living in what seemed like torment in my mind.

So, to get some peace of mind I got the locks changed.

That summer, every chance I got I was at my best friend's house or back home at my grandparents' house. Once school started and I went back to work, I had to be at home more. He finally moved out on October 2nd. The day after our 3-year anniversary. It was supposed to be on our anniversary, I think he did that on purpose. He ended up needing to stay an extra night. He had already moved his stuff out including his bed, so he asked if he could sleep in the bed with me. As much as I didn't want him to, I said yes. I know what you may be thinking, "It's a trap!" But it was strictly sleeping and nothing more.

During that time, I wasn't working because I had gotten a new teaching job. I hadn't started yet, because it was still summertime. So, I had begun to sell art and it sustained me until I started working in August at my new school teaching Kindergarten. I was making enough money from art to keep afloat that summer and he didn't understand how I wasn't struggling being that I didn't have a job at the moment. I don't think he wanted me to struggle, or maybe he did, to show that I needed him and maybe change my mind about leaving.

# CHAPTER THIRTEEN

While I was married, I would always think, "if I were single I'd have more money, my life would be better."

Well, here I am in the middle of a divorce and I, indeed, did not have more money. I was struggling to pay my bills. I began making art during the pandemic in 2020 and that sustained me in the beginning of our separation. The separation left me in a lot of debt. My credit score was better than his, so there were things in my name that he was responsible to pay for, but now were a burden for me once we split.

The weekend that he passed away I went to Raleigh to see three of my closest friends. One of them was visiting from Texas so we went to dinner, talked and caught up. I had just started a new job as a nanny after I left teaching for a brief period.

It wasn't my wisest decision, but I was struggling and could barely afford my dinner. The next morning, I left my friend's house and came back home. It was Saturday and I was preparing for church the next day.

The next day was Sunday, August 21st, 2021. It was a beautiful, sunny day outside with clear blue skies and pure white clouds. I had on a teal blue skirt and a denim shirt.

To earn some extra money, I decided to deliver to Door Dash after church, but first I was going to the mall to get food from the food court. On the way to the mall, I decided to call my grandma and talk to her for a little while. As I was on the phone with my grandmother she got a beep, signaling that someone else was calling her. It was my mother in law. I got curious and wanted to know what his mom was calling about. When my grandma called me back she told me something that would change my life. His mom and grandma had found him deceased in his apartment.

It was his grandmother's birthday, and they were supposed to go out to eat, but he wasn't answering his phone, so they went to his apartment to check on him. That news was something that shook me to my core and not something that I expected to hear anytime soon. It is still sometimes hard to believe that he is no longer alive. When my grandmother told me the news I was in the mall parking lot and all I could do was cry.

I cried and cried hard. I remember saying repeatedly

"I'm sorry, I didn't want this to happen. Why did he have to die?"

I was alone in the parking lot of the mall. So, I texted and called a few friends and one of them sent a mutual friend to get me from the mall. This wasn't the way that I expected things to end as our divorce would be final in a little over a month. The news shocked everyone because it was so unexpected. He was so young. I went from looking forward to closing this chapter in my life and celebrating straight to planning a funeral. I was loud about my new found freedom but now out of respect for him and his family I had to be quiet about it. I didn't want people to mistake my excitement for the new chapter with excitement for how the new chapter unexpectedly began. Contrary to what some people think, this wasn't the closure I wanted.

This made things very complex.

Now, I'm not just grieving the end of a chapter and what I thought my life would be like, but now I'm grieving the physical loss of my husband. It also brought up feelings of grief I carried for the children that I miscarried two years prior.

Here I am, with no husband and no children.

Is this the fresh start that I wanted?

Being that I was still legally married to him, his family

left the planning up to me. I didn't want to do anything. I just wanted to wallow in grief and disbelief. The day it happened, I stayed the night with my mom. She didn't want me to be alone. The next day, I spent the day on the couch. That's where I wanted to stay, but I couldn't. I had a funeral to plan. I had to view his body, give the details for the obituary and everything else.

I just wanted it to be over.

I didn't fight anything. Whatever his family and friends wanted to do I let them. The day of his service, I sat in the front row as his still legal wife. Some people walked past me like I was invisible. Maybe I shouldn't have cared about that, I mean we were almost divorce. But it felt disrespectful. It was time for those that knew and loved him to say a few words.

I said nothing.

Those that did had nothing but the best things to say about who he was. I was glad that they could experience that side of him, but that's not who I knew at home. During that time, I learned that one person's experience of someone doesn't negate someone else's experience of that person. We can have two completely different experiences of the same person.

I knew that his passing wasn't my fault. He passed away

due to diabetic complications. As I mentioned before, we discovered that he was diabetic early in our relationship. He started urinating very frequently. He went to the doctor's, and they told him he was diabetic, but he never accepted it. He continued to eat and drink what he wanted. He never kept track of his blood sugar levels. As a result, he developed cataracts in one of his eyes and had to have the cataracts removed. I tried my best to get him to take it seriously. He would, briefly, and then, would go back into his old habits. Before we conceived I told him that I would not be having children with him until he took his health seriously. That got his attention but only temporarily. This was something that I realized I couldn't care more about than he did. I always had a fear that I would come home and find him in a diabetic coma or something like that. I believe that when we separated he began to care even less about it, which ultimately caused it to get even more out of control.

Even though his death had nothing to do with me, I couldn't help but think that some people connected to him blamed me. Someone even said that they believed he died of a broken heart.

At the time of his passing, I was serving as a greeter at the church I attended. Once a month, we would fast together from different things. This particular time I was fasting from social media, so I hadn't been on social media that entire week. After church that Sunday, I got on Facebook, and I had a few notifications from one of his family members. She and I never had issues so I had no idea that the comments she left on my Facebook posts would be so disgusting. She had gone back to various posts I had posted throughout the year and left disrespectful comments basically blaming me for his death saying things like "I bet you're happy now", "can you forgive yourself for the pain you inflicted." just to name a few of the comments.

As badly as I wanted to respond, the sermon I had just heard, along with the Holy Ghost that lives within me, wouldn't let me respond how I really wanted to. Instead, I blocked her immediately. I can't say that it was easy, because it ate at me for a while. I wanted to tell her how "she had me messed up." Although I didn't tell her how I was feeling, my friends definitely were in the loop. It took a while for me to let it go. I soon realized that she was also hurting and really just needed someone to blame for her pain. What she said no longer stings as much as it once did when I think about it.

It seemed as though I was being swallowed by memories. Right before he passed away I discovered that his job was in the same area as my church. I'd also seen him at a restaurant near my church the week before his untimely passing. I still lived in the townhome that we purchased together where memories still lingered, both good and bad.

Where the dent in the wall was where he threw a can of bug spray toward me because he was angry.

Where one side of the laundry room door was missing because he was angry and accidentally tore it off the hinges.

It was also the place where our friends and family gathered for Christmas and birthdays.

The place where we had prepared to bring our baby home and start a family. The place where some of his belongings still remained.

Where pictures of us still lived.

The place that once was a place of new beginnings was now a reminder of all that I thought I had lost. Almost a year after his passing, I sold the house and went back to renting an apartment. Although it felt good to be a homeowner, selling the house was the closure that I needed to help me move forward.

To give me a fresh start.

To regain the peace that I felt was slipping through my fingers.

For a while I was stuck. I was stuck in what was and

what I wanted. I didn't regret leaving, but unexpectedly becoming a widow had a different impact on me. It was a title that I didn't think I would have for decades to come.

Although we didn't live together when he passed away, for some reason, after his passing, fear tried to grip me. I hated being downstairs once the sun went down. I spent a lot of time upstairs in my bedroom. That lasted a few months and then slowly I would stay downstairs after dark.

My art was also comforting. I was doing art at that time and one of my work spaces was downstairs in my kitchen. That helped me begin to start being ok with being downstairs after dark. I would be working on something and in my groove and I couldn't just stop because the sun had gone down. I had to finish what I was doing. As time went on I slowly began to spend more and more time downstairs until, one day, I wasn't afraid anymore.

# CHAPTER FOURTEEN

I was evolving.

I wasn't the same person that people knew.

They could see the freedom in me. There was a point during the separation that I even questioned my sexuality. If I'm honest, I questioned it before and even during my marriage but now that I was trying to find myself after marriage, I cracked the door a little more. Many people don't know this. I can't even believe I'm writing it. Someone that knew my secret thoughts said they thought I'd date a girl. Even though I had thoughts and questioned my sexuality, I never fully explored it or entertained the thought for very long to act on it. I didn't want to open that can of worms. If you haven't realized it by now I'm a Christian.

Same-sex relationships aren't something that I felt comfortable embracing. Although I respect people's beliefs, sexuality, and things of the like it's not something I wanted for myself. I knew it wasn't what God had for me and I also knew that ultimately I wanted a family with children. Yes you can obtain that in a same sex relationship, but that is not what I wanted for myself. You may be thinking that I wasn't being myself or that I was stifling my desires, but that's also not true. I just decided against walking that path. I didn't just choose the path best for me. I chose the path that God wanted for me.

Once I decided to walk away from my marriage, I couldn't wait until we were officially divorced. I wanted to be in a new relationship very soon after. I've seen where people get remarried quickly after divorce or becoming a widow and I've also seen where they are single for many years before love found them again. I was afraid that maybe the latter would be me but was hoping that God would be quick. You know, "redeem the time."

I wanted my Promised Land to come quickly and didn't want to wait for it too long. I felt as though I'd already wasted so many years in the wrong marriage and I didn't have any more time to waste. I have been reminded that God is not bound by time. He knows better than we do when we are ready for the Promise that God wants to give us. During this time a friend told me "Maybe God is using this season to teach you about patience. You need patience to get you to the promise God has for you. If you rush the promise you are rushing the process. If you rush the process, you'll rush the preparation because the process prepares you for the promise." Patience is essential for the journey.

One day, once again, I was on social media minding my business when I got a DM. It was a guy that I knew of but didn't really know. We had a lot of mutual friends, but that was about it. I was out of town and had posted a picture of me in a super cute, fitting black dress. He liked what he saw. We began chatting and eventually exchanged numbers. We went on one date and talked for a little while after that, but it didn't really go anywhere. After that I didn't date anymore until after my husband had passed away.

About two weeks after burying my husband, it was my church's 5th anniversary, and we had a gathering downtown. I was sitting in my car when a young man came up to my car. I cautiously roll the window down. He told me he liked my car and began asking questions about it. After that he didn't go on about his business he kind of lingered a little and I already knew what was about to happen. He was going to ask for my number. I had just buried my husband two weeks prior, so I was very hesitant. It felt too soon. Well, he asked me if I was single and my response was "Well, I was married. We separated and then he died." I realized this could easily have scared the man off. But it all was so fresh, I didn't know what to do.

Should I have told him now or waited til later?

But it didn't scare him off. He proceeded to ask for my number. Being that I was still trying to navigate being a widow I decided not to give him my number, but to give him my social media handles. He followed me on social media and a few days later he messaged me. We eventually began to date. Everything seemed to be going so well and I actually thought he could be my second chance at love. He was kind, respectful, considerate, among other qualities. Once again, I had a list and he checked off almost all the boxes.

Could this be it? Could this be my second chance at love?

As time went on, I realized I still had some triggers. One Sunday, he was in town visiting as he had moved out of state shortly after we met. I was getting ready for church, and I loved my outfit. I thought I looked cute. He sees what I'm wearing and tells me that he liked the other outfit better. That triggered me. I got upset because the wound from my marriage had not healed from when my husband would criticize what I would wear. He saw that I was upset, and he apologized. He didn't mean that he didn't like what I had on, but he just liked the other outfit better. All my unhealed heart heard was criticism.

We continued to date for a little while after this incident. I was praying for God to show me if he was the one, like I always do when I'm dating because I don't want to waste time. I remember sitting in my car on my lunch break while I was working as a nanny when I began to get this familiar nagging feeling in my heart like I did while I was dating my husband. It made me sad because I'm like here we go again. Things were ultimately going so well, and he checked all my little boxes to the point where I thought maybe he could be "the one."

Did I break it off immediately? No.

I tried to ignore it until one day I just couldn't anymore.

Had I not learned my lesson from the last season?

I didn't want to repeat the mistake, so I made the decision to call it off. He didn't understand at first and kept saying "I've been nothing but nice to you." That was true but being nice to me is the bare minimum. Although I did like him, and even thought that I loved him, I realized that just because he was better than the last didn't mean he was God's best for me. I knew that there was something even better for me than what I was experiencing.

Omesha G.

# CHAPTER FIFTEEN

After that, I didn't have another relationship. It was my goal to really be content in the season I was in. I wanted to continue to serve in my church and grow closer to God and get to know myself more. I don't have a problem doing things by myself, but I wanted to be more intentional about dating myself, to be intentional about getting to know myself more, learning what I liked and disliked. I believe that this is a part of the preparation process on my journey to my promise.

One day, I got a DM from a local pastor that I know. She had a Word from the Lord for me. I won't tell you everything that it said but it confirmed my desire to be married and have children. One of the things she told me is, "Because you have trusted God with your life, He will trust you to carry it! He is stripping you of expectations and checklists concerning your future husband. If you allow Him to strip you of your expectations in the secret place, He will give you His and you will not second guess His son when He sends him to you."

This was a big turning point in my life. It confirmed that God heard my prayers and knows my desires. He is indeed El Roi. He saw me then and still does. I would love to say it has been easy after receiving that Word, that things were smooth sailing. Sometimes, when we receive a Word from God, we like to put our hands in it and try to help him out as if He doesn't know what he's doing. Let's all laugh together.

There was a period where I tried dating apps. They yielded no results for me. At one point, I found myself in a cycle of sin. I had found myself compromising my conviction of remaining abstinent until marriage. I met a guy on a dating app. The first date went really well. I'd like to believe we had a connection. We had a lot in common. As time went on I knew that it wasn't going anywhere. When I asked if he saw us being more than friends, he told me that he wasn't ready for a relationship but once again, like the others previously mentioned I didn't move on. I kept him around. No matter how I tried to spin it we had become just friends with benefits. I mean this man had me weak in the durn knees!

I'd feel convicted. Go to church, cry, repent, tell my friends I'm done, even tell him "We can't see each other anymore. All just to fall back into the same temptation again at some point whether it was a day later, a week later or a month later. I just knew God was sick of me, heck, I was sick of myself. I realized that I couldn't do it on my own, so I reached out to one of the Elders of my church for accountability.

It was the best thing that I could have ever done.

When I reached out to her I knew she meant business. I didn't want to waste her time or disappoint her, and God of course. One thing she told me that made me really take it seriously is that when I reached out to her and explained my situation she said she had a dream that I was pregnant, and I wasn't married.

That was all it took for me.

I was not trying to mess around and find out. Yes, I wanted to be a mom, but I didn't want to be a single mom. I didn't want it if it meant being outside of the Will of God. I wanted my promise. The husband first and then the children. I knew that getting pregnant would further delay God's promise for me. That's the last thing that I wanted to happen.

So, the guy I was seeing at the time was a great guy. Although we had essentially become just friends with benefits he was even better than the last relationship that I had, but again wasn't God's best. I had to make up in my mind that I was not going to settle for anything other than God's best for me. I didn't think he'd understand as we didn't have the same conviction.

Although I didn't reach out to him he would call or text me every other month or so. For some reason I couldn't bring myself to block him. I felt it was a little extreme. After a few months I finally decided to block his number, and social media as well. I realized that keeping that door cracked even a little could possibly get in the way of what God wanted to do.

# CHAPTER SIXTEEN

I had one foot in Egypt and one foot out.

How could God bring me to my Promised Land with one foot still in the wilderness and the bondage of what once was? In the words of Elder Mariah Claiborne, it was time to take off my grave clothes and live. It was time to walk in complete freedom and in anticipation of the Promise that I know God had for me.

This season has seemed like such a long one. I feel like I have lived two separate lives. Sometimes, it is hard to believe that a few short years ago I was married and owned my home. It's hard to believe that I was even pregnant and was almost someone's mom. It was such a hard season, but I refused to let it be in vain. Had I not gone through that time I wouldn't be who I am right now. It has made me a wiser person than I would be had I not gone through any of it.

It has opened my eyes to myself and things I needed to work on. That season brought me closer to God. I had to depend on Him more than I ever had to depend on Him before. Overall, it opened my eyes to things that I now refuse to deal with in a relationship.

I know my worth and what I deserve.

I had to learn the hard way that it is better to obey God the first time, and to not allow disobedience to keep you bound. Acknowledge it, repent and learn from the mistakes so that you don't repeat it. Don't be bound to your mistakes. Disobedience will cause you to go through things that could have been avoided. Had I walked away from the relationship early on I wouldn't have had to experience verbal abuse. I wouldn't have had to experience miscarriages. Maybe I would've had miscarriages later in life with the right person, but who you go through things like that with matters. It can help build you or it can defeat you.

Forgiveness was a big step in moving forward. While I had to forgive him I also had to forgive myself. I had to forgive myself for what I allowed. As we have heard countless times, people only treat you how you allow them to treat you. For a while after the marriage, I beat myself up for what I allowed.

How could I allow someone to treat me that way?

How could I allow someone to talk to me that way?

What would make me stay in a relationship that

long and even go as far as getting married when I knew I shouldn't have married that man?

Then I felt as though I had wasted my grandparents' money. When I first decided to leave, it hurt me to think that my grandparents and my dad put so much money into our wedding for us to not even make it to Year Three. So, I had to take responsibility and forgive him as well as myself so that I could move forward. I knew I couldn't enjoy the new season that I dreamt of for so long if I didn't. I don't want others to think that it was easy because there are times where I had to forgive again.

I saw a post that said, "when you remember, forgive again."

That is something that I had to learn on this journey. Forgiveness won't always be instant and it's not always a "one and done" thing and that is ok. With that, this Journey has consisted of many transitions. Many times, we can be planning and expecting the transition to happen but not the method in which it will happen. One huge transition that I went through on this journey is the transition from married to widow. The death of my husband was one that I did not expect. Yes, the marriage was ending anyway but I was expecting to go from marriage to divorce. Instead, I went from married to widowed in the blink of an eye which meant that my transition came with some grief. I refused to get stuck in transition. As I previously mentioned, I refused to get stuck in the process. This time it wasn't the process of forgiveness but the process of grief. Cry, scream, be angry, feel all the feelings but go through it. Grow through it. Don't allow it to be in vain.

The point is, don't get stuck. Keep moving.

If you don't, you'll never know the beauty of what is on the other side.

If you've ever been through a divorce you can feel like you failed. Especially as a Christian. People can make you feel worse than you already feel if you decide to divorce but not many people get married with divorce in mind. You think and hope that you will be with this person forever. Even with me, knowing that I shouldn't have married the person that I chose, I walked into it only thinking of forever.

So, when it's over and divorce is looking you in the face, it feels like you failed. But there is beauty in closed doors because the ending of something is also the beginning of something new.

"Behold, I will do a new thing; now it shall spring forth; shall ye not know it? I will even make a way in the wilderness and rivers in the desert."

Isaiah 43:19(KJV)

Don't dwell on what was behind the door that closed.

Embrace the new.

A fresh start.

The second chance. What's on the other side of the door could be the answer to what you've been praying for. A big lesson that I learned on this journey has been to trust God. I used to think he wasn't speaking to me but honestly I wasn't spending enough time with him to learn his voice or how he speaks to me. Growing up in church, I know who to pray to when I need direction or answers, but waiting for the answers is what I struggled with. Many times, I would pray and ask God for a "sign", and he would show me the sign but because I didn't like the answer or the answer made me uncomfortable, I would ask for another sign.

As stated previously, I asked for a sign if my husband was the one. He gave me the sign, but it wasn't enough for me, and I kept asking for more signs. Why? Because I didn't like the answer that he gave. I tried to make the answer what I wanted it to be. I didn't trust myself or the holy ghost that lives in me enough to know when or how God speaks to me. So not only is it important to have discernment and learn God's voice for yourself but once you do you have to actually listen. I had a habit of becoming codependent on those that I felt had a better relationship with God or that I felt God spoke to more and I could trust that they hear from God. I'm learning that he speaks to me, too, and what is ultimately for me will find me in due time. It doesn't matter how many times I have messed up or fallen, because God will answer all of my prayers. I have been reminded and encourage that "God had already calculated the mistakes you would make." So don't give up. Your disobedience and your mistakes didn't disqualify your for the promise. Keep going, your promise awaits you.

"And let us not be weary in well-doing: for in due season, we shall reap, if we faint not."

Galatians 6:9 (KJV)

# ABOUT THE AUTHOR

Omesha Gaynor is the author of a children's book titled Beautiful Me and the creator of Kidzpiration, daily affirmation cards for kids. She is a North Carolina native and a graduate of the University of North Carolina Greensboro. She currently resides in Greensboro NC with her cat, Prissy, where she teaches Kindergarten. She spends her free time, outside of teaching children, writing her story and testimony in hopes of touching many lives.